How Things Move

Pulls

Sarah Shannon

Heinemann
LIBRARY

www.heinemannlibrary.co.uk
Visit our website to find out more information about Heinemann Library books.

To order:
 Phone 44 (0) 1865 888066
 Send a fax to 44 (0) 1865 314091
 Visit the Heinemann Bookshop at www.heinemannlibrary.co.uk to browse our catalogue and order online.

Heinemann Library is an imprint of Capstone Global Library Limited, a company incorporated in England and Wales having its registered office at 7 Pilgrim Street, London, EC4V 6LB – Registered company number: 6695582

Heinemann is a registered trademark of Pearson Education Limited, under licence to Capstone Global Library Limited

Text © Capstone Global Library Limited 2009
First published in hardback in 2009
The moral rights of the proprietor have been asserted.

Edited by Siân Smith, Rebecca Rissman, and Charlotte Guillain
Designed by Joanna Hinton-Malivoire
Picture research by Elizabeth Alexander
Production by Duncan Gilbert
Originated by Dot Gradations Ltd
Printed and bound in China by South China Printing Company Ltd

ISBN 978 0 431 19321 2 (hardback)
13 12 11 10 09
10 9 8 7 6 5 4 3 2 1

British Library Cataloguing in Publication Data
Shannon, Sarah
  Pulls. - (How things move)
  1. Energy transfer - Juvenile literature
  I. Title
  531.6'8

Acknowledgements
We would like to thank the following for permission to reproduce photographs: ©Alamy pp.**16** (Neil McAllister), **9** (PhotoAlto), **6** (UpperCut Images); ©Capstone Global Library Ltd. p.**18** (Tudor Photography 2004); ©Corbis pp.**4**, **13** (Frédéric Soltan/Sygma), **15**, **20** (Randy Faris); ©GAP Photos pp.**21** (FhF Greenmedia), **19** (Richard Bloom); ©Getty Images p.**7** (Ron Levine/Riser); ©iStockphoto.com pp.**17** (Benoit Rousseau), **14** (Edyta Linek); ©Photolibrary pp.**8**, **23** (Dan Dalton/Digital Vision), **11** (Digital Vision/Per Breiehagen), **5** (F1 Online), **10** (FogStock LLC), **12** (Huntstock RF)

Cover photograph of huskies reproduced with permission of ©Punchstock (Image Source). Back cover photograph of children on a roundabout reproduced with permission of ©Capstone Global Library Ltd. (Tudor Photography 2004)

Every effort has been made to contact copyright holders of material reproduced in this book. Any omissions will be rectified in subsequent printings if notice is given to the publishers.

Contents

Moving

Things can move in many ways.

Things can move fast or slowly.

Pulls

You can pull things to make them move.

You can pull things towards you.

You can pull a cart to make it move.

You can pull a drawer to make it open.

You can pull yourself up on a climbing wall.

You can pull yourself along on
a rope.

Heavy and light

Heavy things are hard to pull.

A heavy fishing boat is hard to pull.

Light things are easy to pull.

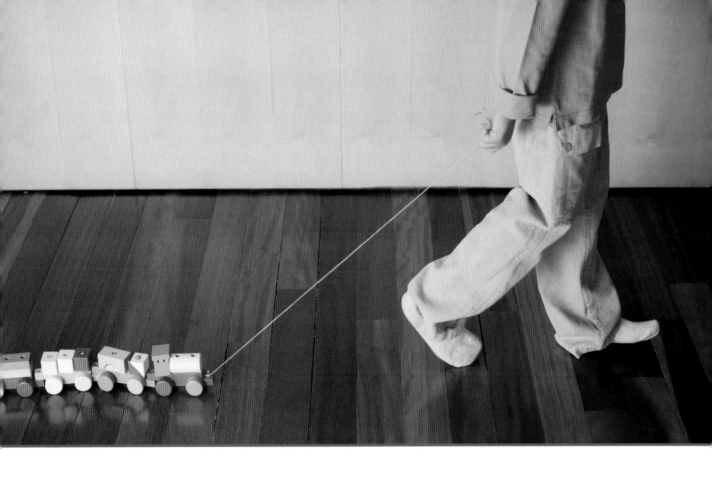

A toy train is easy to pull.

Big pulls

A big pull can make heavy things move.

A big pull can make things
move faster.

Stopping

You can stop things with a pull.

You can stop a trolley with a pull.

Moving things with a pull

A pull can move lots of different things.

What things do you move with a pull?

What have you learned?

- A pull can make something move.

- A pull can make something stop moving.

- A big pull can move heavy things.

- A big pull can make things move faster.

Picture glossary

pull make something move towards you

Index

Notes for parents and teachers
Before reading
Explain to the children that one way of making things move is to pull them. Mime a few actions of pulling (e.g. pulling a brush through your hair, pulling socks on, pulling open a drawer). Ask the children if it is easy to pull a heavy thing or a light thing? Show the children a pull-along toy and ask them how it moves. Is it easier to push it along or to pull it?

After reading
- Blow up a balloon and attach a 1 metre length of wool to the end. Challenge the children to take it in turns to pull the balloon firmly towards them so that it bounces off their heads. Can they do it in one swift pull?
- Tie a 1 metre length of wool to each of three light plastic bricks of equal weight. Take a small toy which is heavier than a brick and tie 1 metre of the same coloured wool to the toy. Make four holes in the lid of a shoe box and thread the pieces of wool through the holes leaving a small length of wool on the outside. Put the items inside the box with the lid on top. Tell the children that there are three light bricks in the box and one heavy toy. Ask a child to pull each string, decide which string they think is attached to the toy and pull this to the top of the box. Find out if they were right. Help them to discover that because the toy is heavier than the bricks, they have to pull the string harder to make it move.
- Sing the song with hand actions: "Wind the bobbin up. Wind the bobbin up. Pull. Pull. Clap, Clap. Clap."